Marty's first Easter Bunny day

Copyright @ Unicorn Love Press. All rights reserved.
No part of this publication may be reproduced, distributed, or transmitted in any form or by any means, including photocopying, recording, or other electronic or mechanical methods, without the prior written permission of the publisher, except in the case of brief quotations embodied in critical reviews and certain other noncommercial uses permitted by copyright law.

Today is a big day for Marty!
He is going to deliver Easter Eggs for the first time ever!

He has been waiting for this day for a long time
He is ready now but he still doesn't know what to expect.

Every time he asked other bunnies how to be an Easter Bunny, they just giggled and said "You'll find out soon!"
It's so frustrating!

He woke up early, showered and was first at the **breakfast** table , before his older siblings were even awake.

As soon as he ate breakfast his mom handed him this tiny little bottle and said Drink it!
What is this, mom?

"It's the Easter Bunny potion. Did you just think the eggs will fall from the sky? Ha Ha"

It was now time to have a little talk

In your first year you will only have 10 eggs. Deliver 9 to your friends. The last one you must bring home to share with us tomorrow at the Easter dinner.

Where do I find the eggs?
You don't find them. They find you! For every Easter Bunny is different. You drank the potion, now it's time to discover your Super Power!

Marty left the house very confused
He was afraid he will fail
at being an Easter Bunny

He made it to the forest and started feeling weird. It was almost as if ...

Pfft
Please don't let me be sick. Not today!

By the time Marty made it out of the forest it was getting louder and he couldn't make it stop! He was *embarrassed*!

He arrived at a beautiful Meadow and decided that he needed to rest. Farting and running can be so *exhausting*! He never knew that...

He was hoping that if he stopped running he will stop farting as well. But it had gotten worse! And he almost forgot...
HE NEEDED AN EGG! The bear's house was close.

He didn't get to finish his thought and he felt push up by
some strange object. It was the most beautiful Easter Egg
he has ever seen!

Did he just poop it? It didn't feel like it!
But where did it come from? He was just sitting here, farting
and thinking that he will be late for his first customer...

Farting? Hmm it stopped! He knew he couldn't be sick
It would've ruined his first day as Easter Bunny. Oh wait!
He has to run to the bear's house to make his first delivery.

Mama-bear and her cub were already waiting for him with a
jar of honey. He was happy to eat some honey as he needed
energy for the rest of the day. Then off he went ...

As soon as he left the Bear's house it started again.
At first a shy one and then it wouldn't stop. Oddly,
they didn't smell bad. They smelled like cotton candy.

This time he couldn't stop to rest, he needed to get to his next customer. The sun was almost above him, so it must be almost noon. And HE NEEDED AN EGG!

And just like that, out of nowhere, with his next jump,
he landed on an egg! It almost knocked him on his back!
A small fart came out and then it got quiet, again.

The Donkeys were happy with their egg and congratulated Marty on becoming an Easter Bunny. They offered to give him a ride to his next customer, but Marty refused politely.

Marty soon figured out that whenever he says he needs an egg, one will appear out of the blue. So he better stand still and wait for it. Running (and farting) while asking for an egg was not a good idea.

The rest of the day went pretty smooth. He delivered 8 of his 9 eggs and was already tired. Being an Easter Bunny is not easy job. All Marty could think about right now was a nap.

Even the smell of cotton candy annoyed him at this point. He gathered his **strength** and finished his last delivery, planning to go back to the meadow to take a short nap on his way home.

Marty immediately fell into a deep sleep, maybe for just a few minutes or maybe he slept for hours. He couldn't tell. But as long as he laid on a side he didn't fart. That was awesome!

But then suddenly he was wide awake. He was flying or so he thought at first. And he couldn't be more wrong! He was like a balloon **deflating** in every possible direction.

He quickly remembered that he still needs an egg. HIS EGG!
And then it hit him. No, no, like literally hit him. Since he was
flying in every direction, the egg landed on top of his head!

Marty was so over this day! He didn't want to be an Easter Bunny anymore! The work was hard and he was tired after all that happened to him today. No more egg deliveries next year! He was heading home.

At home his parents were waiting for him in the door way. They were cheering his return. They couldn't wait to hear his story. This was a big life event for the Easter Bunnies!

He put his egg in the Easter basket and sat on the couch upset.
They all had so many questions for him!
Tell me son, how was your day?
Did you have fun today?
It was horrible! I am glad it's over!
What's your Super Power, little brother?
What's that smell?

I had gas the whole day and it wouldn't stop except during deliveries. It was embarrassing, exhausting and annoying. Being Easter Bunny must be the hardest job on Earth!

Marty's parents looked at each other in shock. They just couldn't believe what Marty just said. Is he ....?
Tell me son, how did they smell like?
Did you spend a lot of time in one place?
They smelled like cotton candy! I spent time in the meadow. Why?
Marty Farty is your new name, bro!
What's going on?

Children, Marty is one in a million Easter Bunny! A myth we didn't think existed. We are going to spend Easter in the Meadow tomorrow. It's going to be the best Easter ever!

Easter Sunday in the Meadow
Do you see now how special you are, Marty?
You did this Marty! With your hard work yesterday.
WOW!!!
So cool!
Where did this come from?

Happy Easter!
Being an Easter Bunny is the best job in the whole world!
I can't wait to do this again next year!

www.ingramcontent.com/pod-product-compliance
Lightning Source LLC
Chambersburg PA
CBHW042057110726
48006CB00002B/427